Ohio Expungement Guide

What You Need to Know For Criminal Record Expungement & Sealing In Ohio

Shawn Dominy, Attorney at Law

Rivers Edge Publishing, LLC

This guide is not legal advice. Although this guide is written by a lawyer and contains useful information about a legal issue, it is not legal advice. Reading the guide does not create an attorney-client relationship. The facts and circumstances of every case are different. For a lawyer to give you legal advice, the lawyer needs to know the facts and circumstances of your particular case. Otherwise, it would be like a doctor performing a medical procedure without knowing your symptoms and medical history. If you want legal advice for your specific case, you should hire a lawyer with expertise in the area of criminal record expungement/sealing.

Laws change. This guide's summary of the Ohio laws for record expungement/sealing is accurate as of the time the guide is written. However, the statutes governing record expungement/sealing may be changed by the Ohio legislature at any time.

ISBN: 978-1-7368732-8-1

Cover Design by: Shawn Dominy
Author Photo by: Klatte Photography

Dedicated to Bryan Hawkins and Windy Renee Hall of the Dominy Law Firm for their invaluable contributions to this guide.

CONTENTS

INTRODUCTION

An isolated mistake shouldn't haunt you forever. People make mistakes, and some mistakes lead to a criminal record. A criminal record is a stigma nobody wants, and it can have a significant impact on your life. Thankfully, most criminal records can be expunged or sealed, meaning the public can no longer view the records. Having records expunged or sealed ends the stigma and negative impact of your criminal record.

People considering record expungement/sealing have questions. Most people are unfamiliar with Ohio's expungement/sealing laws, so they have questions, such as:

- What is the difference between expungement and sealing?
- Is my case eligible for expungement/sealing?
- When can I apply?
- How do I apply?
- What should I expect in court?
- What happens if my records are expunged/sealed?
- Will a sealed/expunged record show-up on a background check?
- Should I hire a lawyer?
- How do I choose a good lawyer?

I wrote this guide to answer those questions. I am a lawyer in Columbus, Ohio, and I have been practicing criminal law for over 25 years. Having represented many clients for record expungement/sealing, I know how empowering it is for my clients to receive answers to their questions. Reading the information in this guide is a great way to have your questions answered.

There is misinformation about record expungement/sealing. Some people believe criminal records in Ohio disappear after a certain time. They don't. Many people have the impression expungement/sealing is automatic. It isn't. Instead, a judge holds a hearing, the prosecution may object, and the judge must determine whether the applicant's interest in having the records expunged/sealed outweigh the government's interest in maintaining the records.

This guide will help. In privacy and comfort, you can have your questions answered by reading this guide. This guide is divided into six parts:

- *Part One* defines record expungement and record sealing and explains the difference between the two.
- *Part Two* addresses the criteria for eligibility and provides the waiting periods for different types of cases.
- *Part Three* describes the court process, including what to expect at the hearing.
- *Part Four* explains what happens when criminal records are expunged/sealed.
- *Part Five* reveals what appears in criminal history checks, including checks done by private background companies.
- *Part Six* provides a framework for determining whether you want to hire a lawyer. If you decide to hire a lawyer, this part contains resources for finding a good one.

My goal in writing this guide is to provide you with the valuable information you should have before applying for criminal record expungement/sealing in Ohio. My hope is that, by reading this guide, you can make well-informed decisions about how to proceed with your case.

Shawn Dominy, Attorney at Law

THIS GUIDE IS NOT LEGAL ADVICE

Although this guide is written by a lawyer and contains useful information about a legal issue, it is not legal advice. Reading the guide does not create an attorney-client relationship. The facts and circumstances of every case are different. For a lawyer to give you legal advice, the lawyer needs to know the facts and circumstances of your particular case. Otherwise, it would be like a doctor performing a medical procedure without knowing your symptoms and medical history. If you want legal advice for your specific case, you should hire a lawyer with expertise in the area of criminal record expungement/sealing.

LAWS CHANGE

This guide's summary of the Ohio laws for record expungement/sealing is accurate as of the time the guide is written. However, the statutes governing record expungement/sealing may be changed by the Ohio legislature at any time.

PART ONE:
WHY EXPUNGE/SEAL CRIMINAL RECORDS

Are Criminal Records Permanent?

When a person is charged with a criminal offense, the charge is written on a 'charging instrument', which may be in the form of a complaint, indictment, or bill of information. One copy of the charging instrument is served on the defendant, and one copy is filed in the Clerk of Court office.

The Clerk of Court office opens a court file. As the case proceeds, case records are maintained in the court file. The case records include the charging instrument, subpoenas, documents filed by the defendant and prosecutor, recordings of testimony and hearings, the judge's entries, and any other records filed in the case.

The case records are permanent. Some people are under the impression case records are not available after a certain time. This is not true. After the case is opened, for the rest of time, any person can view the case records at the Clerk of Court office, on the court's website, or through a public records request. In addition, for the rest of time, a record of the case may appear in a criminal background check.

What is Criminal Record Expungement/Sealing?

Record sealing is the removal of the case records from public view. Sealing records is like locking the records in a filing cabinet. Only certain people have the key to the filing cabinet, and the records in the filing cabinet may only be inspected for limited purposes. Part 4 of this Guide explains who has the key and the limited purposes for which the records may be inspected.

Record expungement means to destroy, delete, and erase the records so the records are permanently irretrievable. Expunging records is like running the records through a shredder (except an expunged conviction may be used in a future criminal proceeding and may be considered for employment in law enforcement).

Although there is a difference between record expungement and record sealing, the result of each is the public cannot view the case records. If a person were to search for expunged/sealed case records at the Clerk of Court office, on the court's website, or through a public records request, the person would not find any records. It would be as though the case never existed.

Why Request Expungement/Sealing?

You would probably like it to be as though your criminal case never existed. Until the records for a criminal case are expunged/sealed, the records do exist. Those records are available to the public, and any person can view those records at the Clerk of Court office, on the court's website, or through a public records request.

The records are also available to companies which provide background checks. When a background check is conducted, the report will likely show the offense(s) with which you were charged, the jurisdiction, and the outcome of the case(s). Having a criminal record appear on a background check can affect many aspects of life, including employment, professional licensing, military service, loans, housing, immigration, and volunteering opportunities.

Individuals have different reasons for wanting to expunge/seal their records. The most common reason people seek expungement/sealing is employment, as most employers use background checks to screen applicants. Some people apply for record expungement/sealing because they simply do not want the stigma of a criminal record following them indefinitely.

Part One has clarified criminal records are permanent if the records are not expunged/sealed. This part has also explained why you may want to have your criminal records expunged/sealed. Before you apply to have your case records expunged/sealed, you want to be sure the case is eligible for expungement/sealing. Eligibility for expungement/sealing is explained in Part Two.

PART TWO: ELIGIBILITY

Types of Case Dispositions

In Ohio, the type of case disposition determines what rules apply for record expungement/sealing. There are two categories of case dispositions.

The first category is convictions and bail forfeitures. A 'conviction' is a finding of guilt. A conviction occurs if a person is found guilty at trial, pleads guilty, or pleads no contest and is found guilty by the court. A 'bail forfeiture' is an agreement between the prosecutor and defendant in which the defendant forfeits bail in exchange for the prosecutor not pursuing the charge(s). Bail forfeitures are only permitted in criminal cases which are misdemeanors.

The second category is not guilty findings, dismissals, no bills, and pardons. A 'not guilty finding' occurs if a person is found not guilty in trial or pleads no contest and is found not guilty by the court. A 'dismissal' (aka 'nolle prosequi') is when a person is charged with an offense and the case is dropped by the prosecution and/or court. A 'no bill' is issued when a grand jury considers an allegation that a person committed an offense and does not issue an indictment charging the person with the alleged offense. A 'pardon' is an order from the governor which relieves a person of all disabilities arising out of a conviction.

It is important to know your type of case disposition so the rules are followed for that category of disposition. The rules determine what cases are eligible for sealing, what cases are eligible for expungement, the waiting period to apply for record sealing, and the waiting period to apply for record expungement. In addition, each category has offenses which are ineligible for expungement/sealing.

Ineligible Offenses-Not Guilty Finding/Dismissal/No Bill/Pardon

Cases which are resolved with a not guilty finding, dismissal, no bill, or pardon are all eligible for record sealing. Most of these cases are also eligible for record expungement. However, record expungement is not available for pardons, and record expungement is not available for not guilty findings/dismissals/no bills involving the following offenses:

- An offense under Ohio Revised Code Chapters 4506, 4507, 4510, 4511, or 4549, or a municipal ordinance substantially similar to any section in those chapters. These offenses are traffic offenses.
- A felony offense of violence that is not sexually oriented. 'Offenses of violence' are listed on page 9.
- A sexually oriented offense when the offender is subject to the requirements of Ohio Revised Code Chapter 2950 (registering as a sex offender).
- An offense in which the victim was less than 13 years of age, except convictions for Nonsupport of Dependents.
- An offense which is a felony of the first degree or second degree.
- An offense which is a violation of Ohio Revised Code section 2919.25 (Domestic Violence) or Ohio Revised Code section 2929.27 (Violating a Protection Order).
- An offense which is a felony of the third degree, if the person has more than one other felony conviction or, if the person has two convictions for felonies of the third degree, the person has more convictions than those two third-degree felonies and two misdemeanors.

For the offenses listed in the bullet points, if the disposition is a not guilty finding/dismissal/no bill, the case records are eligible for sealing but not expungement.

Ineligible Offenses-Conviction/Bail Forfeiture

Criminal cases with a disposition of bail forfeiture are all eligible for both record sealing and record expungement. Most criminal cases with a disposition of conviction are also eligible for both sealing and expungement. However, neither sealing nor expungement are available for convictions involving the following offenses:

- An offense under Ohio Revised Code Chapters 4506, 4507, 4510, 4511, or 4549, or a municipal ordinance substantially similar to any section in those chapters. These offenses are traffic offenses, and convictions for traffic offenses generally cannot be expunged/sealed.
- A felony offense of violence that is not sexually oriented. 'Offenses of violence' are listed on page 9.
- A sexually oriented offense when the offender is subject to the requirements of Ohio Revised Code Chapter 2950 (registering as a sex offender).
- An offense in which the victim was less than 13 years of age, except convictions for Nonsupport of Dependents.
- An offense which is a felony of the first degree or second degree.
- An offense which is a violation of Ohio Revised Code section 2919.25 (Domestic Violence) or Ohio Revised Code section 2929.27 (Violating

a Protection Order).

- An offense which is a felony of the third degree, if the person has more than one other felony conviction or, if the person has two convictions for felonies of the third degree, the person has more convictions than those two third-degree felonies and two misdemeanors.

For the offenses listed in the bullet points, if the disposition is a conviction, the case records are not eligible for sealing or expungement. There is one exception: a fourth-degree misdemeanor Domestic Violence conviction may be sealed but not expunged.

Pending Criminal Proceedings

When a judge is deciding whether to grant an application for record expungement or record sealing, the judge must determine whether criminal proceedings are pending against the applicant. If the applicant has pending criminal proceedings, the judge will not grant the application for expungement or sealing.

OFFENSES OF VIOLENCE

The statutes related to record expungement and record sealing reference 'offense of violence'. Record sealing and expungement are not available for a conviction of a felony 'offense of violence'. Expungement is not available for a dismissal/no bill of a felony 'offense of violence'. As defined in the Ohio Revised Code, 'offense of violence' means any of the following:

2903.01-Aggravated Murder	2907.12-Felonious Sexual Penetration
2903.02-Murder	2909.02-Aggravated Arson
2903.03-Voluntary Manslaughter	2903.03-Arson
2903.04-Involuntary Manslaughter	2909.24-Supporting Act of Terrorism
2903.11-Felonious Assault	2911.01-Aggravated Robbery
2903.12-Aggravated Assault	2911.02-Robbery
2903.13-Assault	2911.11-Aggravated Burglary
2903.15-Permitting Child Abuse	2911.12-Burglary if ¶(A)(1), (2) or (3)
2903.18-Strangulation	2917.01-Inciting to Violence
2903.21-Aggravated Menacing	2917.02-Aggravated Riot
2903.211-Menacing by Stalking	2917.03-Riot
2903.22-Menacing	2917.31-Inducing Panic
2903.34-Patient Neglect if ¶(A)(1)	2917.321-Swatting
2905.01-Kidnapping	2919.22-Endangering Children
2905.02-Abduction	2919.25-Domestic Violence
2905.11-Extortion	2921.03-Intimidation
2905.32-Trafficking in Persons	2921.04-Intimidation of Victim/Witness
2907.02-Rape	2921.34-Escape
2907.03-Sexual Battery	2923.161-Improperly Discharging
2907.05-Gross Sexual Imposition	Firearm into Habitation

Waiting Periods-Not Guilty Finding/Dismissal/No Bill/Pardon

If your case disposition is a finding of not guilty or a dismissal, you may apply for expungement/sealing of the case records at any time after the not guilty finding or dismissal is journalized.

If your case disposition is a no bill, you may apply for expungement/sealing of the case records two years after the no bill is reported by the grand jury to the court.

If your case disposition is a pardon, the waiting period depends on the type of pardon granted. If the pardon is an absolute pardon or a partial pardon, you may apply for sealing of the case records at any time after the pardon is granted. If it is a pardon upon conditions, you may apply for sealing of the case records at any time after all the conditions are met.

WAITING PERIODS FOR ALL CASES ARE SUMMARIZED IN THE TABLE ON PAGE 9

Waiting Periods-Conviction/Bail Forfeiture

The waiting periods for convictions and bail forfeitures depend on the type of case disposition (bail forfeiture or conviction), the type of relief sought (sealing or expungement), and the level of the offense.

If the case disposition is a bail forfeiture, you may apply for *sealing* at any time after the bail forfeiture is journalized. If the level of the offense is a minor misdemeanor, you may apply for expungement six months after the bail forfeiture is journalized. If the level of the offense is not a minor misdemeanor, you may apply for expungement one year after the bail forfeiture is journalized.

If the case disposition is a conviction and the level of the offense is a minor misdemeanor, you may apply for *sealing and expungement* six months after the final discharge.

If the case disposition is a conviction and the level of the offense is a misdemeanor (other than a minor misdemeanor), you may apply for *sealing and expungement* one year after the final discharge.

If the case disposition is a conviction and the level of the offense is a fourth-degree felony or fifth-degree felony, you may apply for *sealing* one year after the final discharge. You may apply for *expungement* 11 years after the final discharge. There is an exception to these waiting periods for a public servant convicted of Soliciting or Accepting Improper Compensation.

If the case disposition is a conviction and the level of the offense is a third-degree felony, you may apply for *sealing* three years after the final discharge. You may apply for *expungement* 13 years after the final discharge. There is an exception to these waiting periods for a public servant convicted of Soliciting or Accepting Improper Compensation.

If the case disposition is a conviction and you were a public servant convicted of Soliciting or Accepting Improper Compensation, you may apply for *sealing and expungement* seven years after the final discharge, unless the conviction is a felony. If the conviction is a felony, you may apply for *expungement* 17 years after the final discharge.

If the case disposition is a conviction and you were subject to the requirements of Ohio Revised Code Chapter 2950 (registering as a sex offender), you may apply for *sealing* five years after the requirements have ended. You may apply for *expungement* ten years after you are eligible for record sealing.

'Final Discharge'. When the case disposition is a conviction, the waiting period begins running upon the 'final discharge'. The 'final discharge' occurs when you satisfy all sentencing requirements. For example, if you were ordered to pay a monetary sanction, the final discharge does not occur until the monetary sanction is paid.

WAITING PERIODS

Disposition=*No* Conviction	**Sealing**	**Expungement**
Not Guilty/Dismissal	After the not guilty finding or dismissal is journalized	After the not guilty finding or dismissal is journalized
No Bill	Two years after the no bill is reported by the grand jury	Two years after the no bill is reported by the grand jury
Pardon	After the pardon is granted and any conditions are met	Pardons are not eligible for expungement
Bail Forfeiture	After the bail forfeiture is journalized	Minor Misdemeanor-6 months Other Misdemeanor-one year

Disposition=Conviction	**Sealing**	**Expungement**
Minor Misdemeanor	Six months	Six months
Other Misdemeanor	One year	One year
4th or 5th Degree Felony	One year	11 years
3rd Degree Felony	Three years	13 years
Soliciting or Accepting Improper Compensation	Seven years	Misdemeanor-seven years Felony-17 years
Subject to Chapter 2950 (registering as a sex offender)	Five years after requirements have ended	Ten years after case is eligible for sealing

Waiting Periods-Multiple Offenses from Same Act

In some cases, a person may be charged with multiple offenses in connection with the same act. For example, if a defendant causes alarm or annoyance to another person by engaging in fighting, and also causes physical harm to the other person by punching them, the defendant may be charged with Disorderly Conduct (a minor misdemeanor) and Assault (a first-degree misdemeanor).

If a defendant is charged with multiple offenses in connection with the same act, and if the charges have different final dispositions, the defendant may not apply for expungement/sealing until the waiting period has expired for all the charges.

In the above example, suppose the defendant's charge of Disorderly Conduct is dismissed, and the defendant is convicted of Assault. Without the Assault conviction, the defendant could apply to have the Disorderly Conduct dismissal expunged immediately after the dismissal is journalized. Due to the Assault conviction, however, the defendant must wait to apply for expungement/sealing of all the charges until the Assault conviction is eligible for expungement/sealing (one year).

If one of the charges resulting from (or in connection with) the same act can never be expunged/sealed, none of the charges can ever be expunged/sealed. If, in the above example, the defendant caused serious physical harm and was convicted of Felonious Assault, that conviction could never be expunged/sealed. That means the dismissed charge of Disorderly Conduct also could never be expunged sealed.

There is an exception for traffic offenses. Ordinarily, traffic offense convictions cannot be expunged/sealed. However, if a defendant is charged with two or more offenses or in connection with the same act and the final disposition of one (and only one) of the charges is a conviction for a traffic offense (under Ohio Revised Code Chapters 4507, 4510, 4511, or 4549), the traffic offense conviction can be expunged/sealed. For this to happen, the other charges must be eligible for expungement/sealing. This exception does not apply if the traffic offense conviction is Operating a Vehicle under the Influence (OVI) or Physical Control of a Vehicle Under while under the Influence.

PART THREE: THE COURT PROCESS

The Application

The Ohio Revised Code states a defendant may "apply" for record expungement/sealing and specifies when an "application" may be filed. However, Ohio law does not define "application", and there is no statewide application used in all courts.

Some courts have model applications available online or in the Clerk of Court office, but many courts do not. If the court has a model application, it should be completed accurately and entirely. If the court does not have a model application, you must create your own application. The application should indicate what relief is sought (expungement or sealing), the offense(s), the case disposition type, the applicable Ohio Revised Code section, the waiting period, and why the case is eligible for expungement/sealing.

Some courts also require you to submit a proposed judgment entry (aka 'court order'). The proposed entry must provide all the information required by the applicable Ohio Revised Code section.

After the Application

After the application is filed, the court notifies the prosecuting attorney of the application. If the case disposition is a conviction or bail forfeiture, the prosecutor must notify the victim, if applicable. The prosecuting attorney may file a written objection. There is a deadline for filing the objection, and the prosecutor cannot object at the hearing unless the prosecutor files a written objection before the deadline. Any victim may also file a written objection. Unlike the prosecuting attorney, a victim may object at the hearing without having filed a written objection.

The court may have a probation officer prepare a written report. The report contains information about the applicant and the underlying case. The court then schedules a hearing, which must be held between 45 days and 90 days after the application is filed.

The Court Hearing

At the hearing on an application for expungement/sealing, the judge decides whether to grant the application. Before reaching that decision, the judge first determines if the case is statutorily eligible for expungement/sealing, whether the waiting period has expired, and whether the applicant has pending criminal proceedings.

The judge next evaluates whether the applicant has been satisfactorily rehabilitated and considers any objection by the prosecuting attorney and/or victim. Finally, the judge weighs the applicant's interest in expunging/sealing the case records against the government's interest in maintaining the records. The judge then decides whether to grant the application.

The Court Order

If the judge decides to grant the application, the judge issues an entry (aka 'court order'). The entry orders that all official records pertaining to the case be expunged/sealed. The entry also orders that the proceedings in the case are deemed not to have occurred, subject to some exceptions. Those exceptions are explained in Part Four.

PART FOUR: WHAT HAPPENS WHEN RECORDS ARE EXPUNGED/SEALED

When a judge issues an entry granting an application for expungement/sealing, the entry is delivered to the investigating law enforcement agency, the Ohio Bureau of Criminal Investigation, and any public office which may have a record of the case. The entry orders that the official records be expunged or sealed. The recipients must then expunge or seal the official records, and the records generally cannot be disclosed, inspected, or otherwise used.

There are two caveats. First, the court order applies to "official records", and there are some records which are not considered "official records". Second, there are limited purposes for which expunged/sealed records may be used.

What Records *Are* Expunged/Sealed – Official Records

A judge's entry granting expungement/sealing orders that all "official records" be expunged or sealed. "Official records" which are expunged/sealed include the court files, the notation to the case in the criminal docket, subpoenas, documents filed by the defendant or the prosecutor, records of testimony and evidence, entries, affidavits, electronic records, indices, fingerprints and photographs, DNA specimens/records/profiles, law enforcement investigative reports, other investigative reports, and public records that relate to a certificate of qualification for employment.

What Records Are *Not* Expunged/Sealed – Exceptions to Official Records

The following records are not expunged/sealed because these records are exceptions to the definition of "official records":

- Records maintained by a public children services agency or the department of job and family services regarding child abuse or neglect.

- Reports of an investigation maintained by the inspector general regarding investigations of state agencies/officers/employees.
- Records maintained by the state auditor regarding audits and investigations involving state agencies.
- 'Investigatory work product' of a law enforcement officer.

Regarding 'investigatory work product', the law enforcement officers must deliver the work product records to the law enforcement agency. The law enforcement agency must treat the records as if they never existed, except the records may be provided to another law enforcement agency investigating a similar offense. An officer or agency which uses the records for any other purpose can be prosecuted for Divulging Confidential Information.

Purposes for Which Expunged/Sealed Records May be Used

Expunged records may be used for the following purposes:

- The Bureau of Criminal Investigation may keep an expunged record of a conviction and disclose it to law enforcement for the purpose of determining an individual's qualification for employment in law enforcement.
- A prosecutor may use an expunged record of a conviction in a future trial if the conviction is otherwise admissible.
- A board of education is permitted to receive and maintain records of an expunged conviction if it was used as a basis for a student's permanent exclusion.
- The state auditor is permitted to receive and maintain records of an expunged conviction if the conviction was used as a basis for the person's disqualification from holding public office, employment, or position of trust.

Sealed records may be used for the following purposes:

- A law enforcement officer or prosecutor may inspect sealed records to determine whether the nature and character of the offense with which a person is to be charged would be affected by virtue of the person's previously having been convicted of a crime.
- The parole or probation officer supervising a person may inspect sealed records while the person is on parole, community control, or post-release control.
- The person who is the subject of the records or a legal representative of that person may inspect sealed records.
- A law enforcement officer involved in the case may inspect sealed records in defense of a civil action arising out of the officer's involvement in that case.
- A prosecuting attorney may inspect sealed records to determine a

defendant's eligibility to enter a pre-trial diversion program.

- A law enforcement agency, the department of rehabilitation and correction, and the department of youth services may inspect sealed records as part of the background investigation of a person who applies for employment with one of those agencies.
- A law enforcement agency may provide sealed records to another law enforcement agency investigating a similar offense.
- The Bureau of Criminal Investigation may provide sealed records to a board or person for determining employment in certain fields, such as education, developmental disabilities, home health care, childcare, after-school programs, children services, adult daycare, long-term healthcare, and pediatric respite care.
- The Bureau of Criminal Investigation may provide sealed records if the person applies for a peace officer training certificate.
- The Bureau of Criminal Investigation may provide sealed records for determining eligibility for certain types of employment, listed in Ohio Revised Code section 109.572(B).
- The Bureau of Criminal Investigation or a sheriff's office may inspect sealed records regarding an application for a concealed handgun license.
- The attorney general or a court may inspect sealed records for the purpose of determining a person's classification as a sex offender.
- A court, a law enforcement officer, and the BMV may inspect sealed records for the purpose of assessing points against a person's driver's license. Sealing the record of a traffic offense does not erase points assessed to a driver's license.
- A prosecuting attorney or court may inspect sealed records when the nature and character of the offense with which a person is to be charged would be affected by the information.
- A judge may consider a sealed conviction or bail forfeiture in determining the sentence if the applicant is later convicted of another crime.
- A public office may maintain a sealed record for the purpose of compiling statistical data. The record must not contain a reference to the person who is the subject of the case.
- A governmental office which maintains sealed records of convictions or bail forfeitures may maintain an index of the sealed records and make the index available for the purposes listed above.

PART FIVE: BACKGROUND CHECKS

You may be concerned about your criminal record appearing on a background check. Background checks for criminal history are often misunderstood. This section explains how criminal history checks are conducted and the problem which can arise when a private background company conducts a criminal history check.

'National' Criminal History Checks

There is no official national database of criminal records available to the public. While there are national governmental databases of criminal records, such as the National Instant Criminal Background Check System (NICS) and the Criminal Justice Information System (CJIS), members of the public generally cannot access those databases.

Likewise, FBI record checks are generally unavailable to the public. The FBI maintains national criminal record databases as part of the National Crime Information Center (NCIC). Those records are only available to law enforcement agencies and governmental criminal justice agencies. Although individuals can obtain FBI criminal history reports on themselves, most individuals and private entities cannot obtain an FBI criminal history report on someone else. There are exceptions for entities such as schools, licensing boards, and childcare providers.

How Criminal History Checks are Conducted

Criminal history checks are typically conducted in one of two ways. The first way is do-it-yourself (DIY): an individual or entity personally checks public records to find records of a person's criminal history. The second way is hiring a private background check company to check public and private databases to find records of a person's criminal history.

Do-It-Yourself (DIY) Criminal History Checks

One DIY method of conducting a criminal history check in Ohio is to send the subject's fingerprints to the Ohio Bureau of Criminal Investigation (BCI). BCI compares the submitted fingerprints to prints in fingerprint databases and prepares a criminal history report. BCI does not conduct criminal history checks by name, date of birth, or social security number: they only use fingerprints. An individual or entity who wants to do a BCI background check must have the individual get fingerprinted and then submit the fingerprints to BCI.

Another DIY method of conducting a criminal history check in Ohio is to inspect the records of individual courts. Courts maintain public records of criminal cases, and most courts make those records available on a searchable online database. An individual or entity can search the databases of individual courts and can also search the physical court records in person. The records retrieved are limited to the sources searched.

Private Company Criminal History Checks

The time-consuming DIY method only produces records from the specific sources searched, and there is no national database of criminal records available to the public. Therefore, employers and other entities often hire a private background check company to conduct a criminal history check. There are hundreds of private background check companies which provide criminal history checks.

Some private background check companies maintain their own databases of criminal records. Those companies use automated tools to periodically 'scrape' the databases of courts and other agencies throughout the nation and add the data to the company's private database. The number of sources scraped, and the frequency of database updates, varies among companies. The scraping technology is used primarily by larger background check companies, and their data is often sold to smaller background check companies.

Private Criminal History Checks and Expunged/Sealed Records

Most background check companies are regulated by the Federal Fair Credit Reporting Act. According to that law, those companies cannot disclose information about cases which they know have been expunged or sealed.

For a person who has their criminal records expunged/sealed, a problem can arise when a criminal history check is conducted by a private background check company. The background check companies are not required to update their databases with any certain frequency. They are free to update their databases every year or even every two years.

Suppose a person has the official records expunged for a criminal conviction and a prospective employer has a criminal history check done three months later by a background check company. If that company has not updated its database in the last three months, the database will still show the person's conviction. The criminal history report provided to the prospective employer will show the conviction, even though it has been expunged.

To avoid this problem, it is important to have the expungement/sealing entry delivered to background check companies. At the Dominy Law Firm, we have the expungement/sealing entry delivered to over 500 background check companies.

PART SIX: HIRING A LAWYER

Should I Hire a Lawyer?

It is not necessary to hire a lawyer for record expungement/sealing: it is something you can do yourself. Similarly, it is not necessary for me to hire a plumber for a minor plumbing job: it is something I can do myself.

Nevertheless, I hire a plumber because I want to make sure the job is done correctly. If there are complications with the job, I want an experienced professional to address the complications. Hiring a professional also saves me time and relieves possible stress.

If you are seeking expungement/sealing of criminal records, it may be worth hiring a lawyer for the following reasons:

- to guarantee your case is eligible for expungement/sealing
- to ensure the rules are followed for the category of case disposition
- to properly complete and file the application and proposed entry
- to address any objections by the prosecutor and/or victim
- to speak on your behalf at the hearing
- to explain why your interests outweigh the interests of the government
- to deliver the expungement/sealing order to private background check companies.

Each person seeking record expungement/sealing should do a cost-benefit analysis: is it worth paying the lawyer's fee for the reasons listed above.

If you decide to hire a lawyer for criminal record expungement/sealing, you are probably wondering if all lawyers are essentially the same.

Are All Lawyers the Same?

If you are an NFL team owner, does it matter who plays quarterback for your team? Although all the NFL quarterbacks are good, some are better than others. The same is true with lawyers: some are better than others at representing clients for criminal record expungement/sealing. If you are seeking record expungement/sealing, it does matter who represents you. All lawyers are not the same.

How Do I Choose a Good Lawyer?

If you decide to hire a lawyer for criminal record expungement/sealing, you want to hire a good one. But how do you choose a good one? The following tools will assist you in finding a good expungement lawyer:

- Resources for researching lawyers
- Traits to look for in a lawyer
- Questions to ask a lawyer

Resources for Researching Lawyers

Ohio Supreme Court: Every lawyer in the state of Ohio is required to register with the Ohio Supreme Court. You can verify that a prospective lawyer currently is licensed to practice in Ohio, and you can determine if the lawyer has been disciplined by conducting an 'attorney information search'.

Avvo.com: Avvo® is a website designed to help consumers research lawyers. The site contains profiles of most lawyers in Ohio, and each lawyer is given a rating between 1.0 and 10.0. Each profile contains the lawyer's resume and includes client reviews and peer endorsements. You can search for lawyers by practice area and geographic area on the page titled 'Find A Lawyer'.

Lawyer Directory Websites: There are many websites which have lawyer directories. Some of them are for all types of lawyers, and some of them are for criminal defense lawyers. Most directories are not very valuable because they do not really tell you objectively who the best lawyers are. The exceptions are: Super Lawyers®, Martindale-Hubbell®, and Best Lawyers in America®.

Traits to Look for in a Lawyer

1. Focus. Choose a lawyer whose practice is focused on criminal defense. There are hundreds of lawyers in Central Ohio who will represent you for record expungement/sealing. Most of them, however, also practice other areas of law. If you were having a medical problem with your foot, would you hire a family doctor with a general practice, or would you hire a foot doctor?
2. Expertise. Select a lawyer with expertise in record/expungement sealing. Some lawyers know the basics, while others have a deeper understanding of the details.
3. Experience. Hire a lawyer with experience. Some lawyers occasionally handle an expungement/sealing matter, while others do it regularly. Most do not know how to submit expungement/sealing orders to background check companies.
4. Industry recognition. Select a lawyer who is recognized by his or her peers as a leader in criminal defense. Those lawyers are also often

selected for Super Lawyers® and Best Lawyers in America®. In addition, peer reviews are available on Avvo.com.

5. Service. Choose a lawyer who provides good customer service. The number one complaint about lawyers is they do not communicate well with their clients. Your lawyer should keep you updated regarding all developments in your case, provide you with documents related to your case, and answer all your questions. You can expect better service from a lawyer who accepts fewer cases rather than a lawyer with a high-volume practice.
6. Results. Choose a lawyer who has a history of obtaining good results for clients. A lawyer should be willing to publish, or at least share with you, the results of cases similar to yours.
7. Client satisfaction. Find a lawyer who has satisfied clients. Client testimonials are available on many lawyers' websites. An even better source, Avvo.com, is an independent third party that collects reviews from clients and rates lawyers. Hire a lawyer with high ratings from previous clients.
8. Appropriate fees. Select a lawyer who charges appropriate fees. You can find inexpensive representation, but a lawyer who charges low fees either does not intend to do all the work necessary or does not have the expertise and experience to get good results. A low fee may also indicate what the lawyer thinks about the value of his or her service.

Questions to Ask a Lawyer

1. What percentage of your practice is criminal defense?
2. What are the relevant statutes for record expungement/sealing?
3. How many expungement/sealing cases have you handled?
4. How have you been recognized by your peers as a leader in criminal defense?
5. How do you communicate with your clients and how frequently?
6. Have you obtained favorable results in cases like mine?
7. Where can I read reviews about you, other than your website?
8. How much is your fee and what does it include?
9. Do you submit the entry to background check companies

CONCLUSION

You made a great decision to read this guide. Unlike most people seeking criminal record expungement or sealing, you are not in the dark.

This guide provides the information you need before applying for record expungement/sealing. You now understand the basics of expungement/sealing, including the types of case dispositions, criteria for eligibility, and the waiting periods for the different types of cases.

You have an overview of the court process for expunging/sealing criminal records. You are now familiar with the application, what happens after the application is filed, and what to expect at the court hearing. You also understand what happens when records are expunged/sealed, including the limited purposes for which expunged/sealed records may be used. Importantly, you are also aware of how records appear on criminal history checks.

This guide has given you a framework to help you decide whether you want to hire a lawyer to help you expunge or seal your records. If you choose to hire a lawyer, you now have resources for researching lawyers, criteria to evaluate their qualifications, and questions to ask when you speak with them.

If you are concerned about the stigma of your criminal record, don't let it haunt you indefinitely. Using the resources in this guide, you will make well-reasoned decisions about how to handle your expungement/sealing case. If you decide to hire a lawyer, you will be able to find a lawyer with the qualifications to effectively assist you.

ABOUT THE AUTHOR

Shawn Dominy, Attorney at Law

I have practiced criminal defense since 1997. In my practice, I have represented clients for nearly every type of criminal case, from traffic offenses to murder. My experience with criminal cases includes representing many clients for criminal record expungement/sealing.

In 2012, I filed an application to have case records sealed for a family member. Over the prosecutor's objection, the application was granted. However, the prosecution appealed the case. After briefs and oral arguments, the Court of Appeals affirmed the judge's decision to seal the case records.

The experience with my family member's case got me more interested in record expungement/sealing. The more I learned about the intricacies of Ohio laws for these types of cases, the more I enjoyed this area of my practice. I now regularly represent clients for criminal record expungement/sealing.

I am recognized as a leader in Ohio criminal law. I am the past President of the Ohio Association of Criminal Defense Lawyers, and I am listed in Super Lawyers® and Best Lawyers in America® for the area of criminal defense. My law firm is named in Best Law Firms in America®.

My firm limits the number of cases we accept so we can work on each case thoroughly and give every client the service and attention we would want as a client. We only represent clients in Central Ohio courts, and we only practice criminal defense, including record expungement/sealing.

You can learn more about my law firm on our website. If you finish your research and would like to discuss representation, you can schedule a free phone consultation by completing a contact form on the website or by calling the Dominy Law Firm at 614-717-1177.

Made in United States
Orlando, FL
04 November 2026

90203681R00016